Eat well, feel great

Colourful and delicious meals and snacks

Whether you live on your own, or occasionally find yourself cooking a meal for yourself, this book is filled with colourful and delicious recipes for every occasion.

These recipes are meals for one, but they can easily be increased to serve more. Where the recipe makes a larger amount, the food can be stored in the fridge for a few days or frozen for another day. Some recipes, such as the fresh pesto will keep in the fridge for one month.

We have included healthy and tasty versions of traditional favourites and also hope to introduce you to some new dishes that are quick and easy to make. We have provided suggestions for alternative ingredients to make them interesting and varied. We hope you will enjoy preparing and eating these dishes as much as we do.

50 delicious recipes for all occasions

Recipes

Seasoning

Breakfasts

Light meals / snacks

Salads

Vegetables

Beef dishes

Chicken dishes

Fish dishes

Pork and other meats

Sweets and desserts

Recipes marked with the symbol (V) are suitable for vegetarians.

How to eat well and feel great in later life

In later life, our bodies are less efficient at absorbing the goodness from our food so it is important to eat regularly through the day to maintain energy levels and make sure we get the nutrition we need. As we get older, our muscle size decreases, appetites become smaller and our bodies are less efficient at absorbing vitamins and minerals from our food. We are more vulnerable to viruses and bacterial infections as our body's ability to fight and recover from infection reduces with age. A balanced healthy diet provides the nutrition needed to protect our bodies and reduce the risk of getting viruses and bacterial infections.

Proteins

These recipes include plenty of ideas for enjoying meat, poultry, fish, eggs and pulses. These protein foods help the body fight infection and promote recovery from illness. Fish, in particular, is a good source of protein and is low in saturated fat. Oily fish (such as salmon, fresh tuna, herring, mackerel, pilchards and sardines) contain vitamin A (good for eyes and skin) and D (an important vitamin used in the body to absorb calcium) and omega 3 fats which reduce the risk of heart disease, stroke and inflammation. Aim to have oily fish once a week. Pulses (such as peas, beans and lentils) are also rich in fibre, which encourages a healthy digestive system and can protect against heart disease.

Season without salt

Sensitivity to taste declines with age and adding more salt to increase flavour can be habit forming. However health conditions such as high blood pressure, increased risk of heart disease and stroke are linked to consuming too much salt. Aim to consume no more than 6g (1 teaspoon) of salt each day. This includes salt in processed foods as well as salt added while cooking and at the table. The first recipe in this book is for an easy to make salt free seasoning mix. Once made it will store in a jar and can be used in place of seasoning in all dishes. Feel free to experiment with the spices and herbs to create your own personal seasoning mix that suits you.

Fruit and vegetables

The dishes in this book are full of colour, taste and
texture. You will find plenty of suggestions for great ways
to enjoy fruit and vegetables, a great source of vitamins
and minerals, natural fibre and low in fat. All fruit and
vegetables are good for us, whether they are fresh, frozen,
dried, tinned, cooked or raw. They all have good nutritional
value. A wide variety included in meals and snacks will
mean you get plenty of benefits. Leafy green vegetables
provide iron to oxygenate the blood and folate which
promotes healthy hearts. A small glass of orange juice with
a meal will help the body absorb the iron in your food. If you
are cooking for one you may find it easier to buy fruit and
vegetables loose rather than in large bags to save money
and avoid waste. Instead of choosing onions, you may find
shallots a better alternative, as they are smaller.

Sugars

Most of us enjoy a sweet treat. However there is absolutely no requirement for and no
benefit of, added sugars to older people. We can get our energy from all the other foods
we eat. Although sugars give us calories, do not confuse that with 'get up and go' energy.
Added sugars have been linked with weight gain, obesity, diabetes and tooth decay. If you
are having yoghurt, choose natural yoghurt rather than pre-flavoured ones and add a little of
your own honey or sugar. It is not that honey or sugar is okay, but if you sweeten it yourself,
you have more control over the amount of sugar added. If you are eating sugary food, then
enjoy it as part of a larger meal. The sugar then takes longer to be digested (so you will feel
fuller) and reduces the damage that the sugar can cause to our teeth.

Carbohydrates

You will find plenty of recipes in this book to help you enjoy carbohydrate foods such as
potatoes, rice, pasta and grains. These starchy foods provide us with slow release energy, are
naturally low in fat and a good source of B vitamins, especially important for a healthy nervous
system. Wholegrain starchy carbohydrates such as brown or wholegrain rice and wholemeal
versions of bread and pasta are great sources of fibre, which can lower the risk of heart
disease, encourage a healthy digestive system and reduce constipation.

Vary your carbohydrates every day. Choose porridge for a healthy breakfast or have whole oats
with fruit and yoghurt. Have oatcakes instead of crackers with cheese for a snack. Try sweet
potatoes mashed or baked in the oven. When making mashed potato, include sweet potato or

parsnips, or add a few drops of olive oil and fresh rosemary for an aromatic Mediterranean mash. Consider trying different grains such as couscous or bulgar wheat. Buy them dried or ready to eat and enjoy with grilled meat, salmon or trout. Cook jacket potatoes in the microwave, or for a crispier skin cook for a few minutes in the microwave and finish cooking in the oven.

If you are happy with your weight, 40 per cent of your plate should contain starchy carbohydrate foods. If you are trying to lose weight, keep starchy carbohydrates plain and to one third of your plate and replace with fruit and vegetables. If you are underweight, struggling to maintain weight or your appetite is small consider enriching your meals. You can do this by adding things such as butter, margarine, mayonnaise and olive oil to your mashed potato or pasta. These increase the calories and the energy content, whilst also making your food more tempting and tasty.

Dairy

Dairy foods are a good source of protein, B Vitamins and calcium, which helps keep bones healthy. Whilst rich in calcium, the fat in cheese is saturated fat. If you are trying to lose weight choose 'reduced fat' or 'lighter' types of cheese. Choose low fat yoghurts wherever possible and try fat free yoghurt. When buying flavoured yoghurts, watch out for added sugars. Add your own fruit to fat free yoghurts rather than buying yoghurts with added sugar and fruit.

Oils and fats

We all need oil and fat in our diet so do not aim to have a fat free diet. However, some fats are better for our health than others. Saturated fat is linked to high cholesterol levels, heart disease and strokes. Unsaturated fats are also found in oily fish, nuts (especially almonds, hazelnuts and walnuts), sunflower seeds and avocados. They can help to lower cholesterol when substituted for saturated fats. By exchanging saturated fat for unsaturated fat, we can achieve a better balance for our health. Rather than using lard in cooking, try using olive oil, sunflower oil, sesame oil or rapeseed oil. They have the same calories but are better for your health and heart. Choose spreads with added omega 3 oils in them or with olive oil. It is important to remember that meat naturally contains fat. Where possible choose lean cuts of red meat (beef, pork, lamb) and trim off the visible (saturated) fat before cooking. If you are overweight and trying to lose weight, then cutting down on your fat intake can help greatly. If your appetite is low then try eating nuts, oily fish and using olive oil.

A balanced healthy diet provides the nutrition needed to protect our bodies and reduce the risk of getting viruses and bacterial infections.

Suggested store cupboard ingredients

Having food in your cupboards, fridge and freezer means more choice when you do not want to do a lot of cooking or go shopping.

Cupboard

- Selection of seasonings, herbs and spices (Italian mixed herbs / oregano / rosemary / chilli powder / cinnamon / cayenne / paprika / mixed spice / black and white pepper)
- Stock cubes or powder (chicken, beef and vegetable)
- Bottle of olive oil and sunflower oil
- Tinned fruit such as pears or peaches (look for fruit in juice rather than syrup)
- Tins of vegetables and beans such as tomatoes, baked beans, butter beans, kidney beans, peas, and sweetcorn
- Tinned fish such as tuna, sardines or salmon
- Honey
- Ready to eat dried fruits (apricots, prunes, and sultanas)
- Porridge oats
- Packets of pulses such as lentils and barley
- Packets of rice, pasta shapes and couscous
- Plain flour
- Cartons of evaporated milk, long life milk, and ready-made custard
- Oatcakes or wholegrain crackers (enjoy with cheese or fish paté)
- Eggs

Fridge

- Polyunsaturated spread (less than 70% fat) e.g. olive oil spread
- Low fat mayonnaise
- Jar of your favourite chutney or pickle
- Mustard – French and English
- Cheese

Freezer

- Frozen berries ready for a dessert with yoghurt or custard
- Frozen ready prepared vegetables including peas, beans, carrots, and potato products
- Try to keep a loaf of bread in the freezer (separate the loaf into 2-4 slices)

Notes

Our recipes have been designed to use store cupboard ingredients and basic kitchen equipment easily available to buy. You may find a stick blender is useful for making breadcrumbs and creating smooth soups and sauces and a set of kitchen scales will help with measuring.

Vegetarian recipes – Recipes marked with the symbol (V) are suitable for vegetarians.

Low fat spread – Where a recipe states low fat spread, it refers to vegetable fat-based spreads containing unsaturated fats. Refer to product packaging to check if they can be used for baking.

Egg size – All recipes use medium sized eggs.

Recipe timings – These are approximate to provide guidance.

All the recipes use the symbol ⧖ as guidance.

⧖   **Quick and easy recipe**
⧖⧖   **Need a little more time**
⧖⧖⧖ **More time and attention needed**

Salt free seasoning (V)
Preparation time 10 minutes

Use this blend of herbs and spices to add flavour to dishes instead of salt.

Method

1. Combine **all the ingredients** and mix well.
2. Store in an airtight container for up to 6 months.

Ingredients

5 teaspoons onion powder

2½ teaspoons garlic powder

2½ teaspoons sweet paprika

2½ teaspoons dry mustard

1½ teaspoons thyme or Italian mixed herbs

1 teaspoon black pepper

1 teaspoon cayenne pepper (optional)

Homemade pesto (V)

Preparation time 10 minutes

Method

1. Add **pine nuts, basil, cheese, olive oil** and **garlic** to a food processor or into a jug for a stick blender.
2. Blend until smooth.
3. Season to taste.

Ingredients

50g (2oz) pine nuts
100g (4oz) fresh basil
25g (1oz) parmesan cheese
150ml (¼ pint) olive oil
2 garlic cloves

Makes 250ml (10 fl oz) or 5 servings when used as a pasta sauce. This pesto can be stored in the fridge in a jar for up to a month.

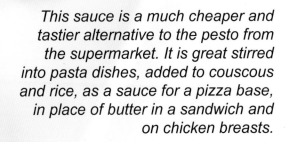

This sauce is a much cheaper and tastier alternative to the pesto from the supermarket. It is great stirred into pasta dishes, added to couscous and rice, as a sauce for a pizza base, in place of butter in a sandwich and on chicken breasts.

For a different take on this pesto, why not substitute the basil for some sun-dried tomatoes. Another alternative is to use garden peas in place of the pine nuts and mint in place of the basil.

Fruit smoothies (V)
Preparation time 5-10 minutes

Most smoothies follow the same basic principle and smoothie making is all about experimenting with different flavours to come up with your favourite combinations of ingredients. Blend solid ingredients (fruit, oats, nuts) together until smooth then add the liquid (juice, milk, yoghurt, honey) until the smoothie is the consistency of your choice. Why not try mango, pomegranate or grape juice?

Method

1. Wash and dry the **fresh fruits**. Add the **fruit**, some of the **juice** and **vanilla extract** (if using) into a food processor or jug to use with a stick blender.
2. Blend for a minute or two until completely smooth.
3. Add the fruit juice until the smoothie is the consistency you require.
4. Pour into your glass of choice and enjoy.

Banana Berry smoothie
Ingredients (Serves 1)
1 small ripe banana
140g (5oz) blackberries, blueberries, raspberries or strawberries (fresh, frozen or tinned fruit in juice)
50ml (2 fl oz) of apple juice

Peach Melba smoothie
Ingredients (Serves 1)
100g (4oz) peach halves
50g (2oz) raspberries (fresh, frozen or tinned fruit in juice)
50ml (2 fl oz) orange juice
1 drop of vanilla extract

Compote of dried fruits (V)

Preparation time 5 minutes

Cooking time 10 minutes

Method

1. Place **fruits, orange juice** and **honey** (if using) in a pan, bring to the boil and simmer gently on a low heat for 10 minutes until the fruit has softened. Stir occasionally to make sure it stays moist.
2. Cover and leave to cool.

Ingredients

250g (10oz) ready to eat dried fruits (apricots, mango, prunes, sultanas, pineapple)

150ml (5 fl oz) orange juice

1 teaspoon honey (optional)

Store in a jar or plastic food storage container for up to a week.

This is delicious topped with plain yoghurt or as an accompaniment to porridge.

Fruity porridge (V)

Preparation time 5 minutes

Cooking time 5 minutes

Tastes good at any time of the day.

Try it with a spoonful of compote of dried fruits (see page 13).

Method

1. Place **oats, milk** and **salt** (if using) into a small saucepan.
2. Bring slowly to the boil, stirring continuously.
3. Once boiling, reduce heat and simmer gently for 2–3 minutes.
4. Serve with **cold milk**.
5. Top with sliced **banana, berries** or **sultanas.**

Ingredients

50g (2oz) porridge oats

250ml (10 fl oz) of milk (or use ½ milk and ½ water)

A pinch of salt (optional)

1 ripe banana, sliced or mashed or 25g (1oz) berries or sultanas

A little cold milk for serving

Cinnamon French toast with fruit (V)

Preparation time 5 minutes

Cooking time 5-10 minutes

Method

1. Put the **egg, cinnamon** and **milk** in a wide, shallow bowl and beat well.
2. Immerse the **bread** in the egg mixture, turning once, until all of it is absorbed.
3. Heat a non-stick frying pan using a medium heat and cook the bread for 2–3 minutes on each side, or until golden-brown. Use 2 teaspoons **olive oil** if needed.
4. Serve the toast on a plate with the **soft fruit**.

Ingredients

1 egg

A pinch of cinnamon

25ml (2 tablespoons) skimmed or semi-skimmed milk

1 slice of thick-cut bread (stale is best) (wholemeal or seeded if you have it)

100g (4oz) fresh, frozen or tinned soft fruit: strawberries, blueberries or raspberries

2 teaspoons olive oil

Tomato and vegetable soup (V)

Preparation time 10 minutes

Cooking time 45 minutes

The soup tastes even better the next day. Remember to bring it back to the boil for at least 5 minutes.

Method

1. Heat the **olive oil** in a heavy based pan.
2. Add the **onion, celery, carrot, leek, potato** and **garlic** and stir over a medium heat for 5 minutes.
3. Add the **tomatoes, stock** and **seasoning**.
4. Bring to the boil (stirring occasionally). Turn the heat low, cover and leave to cook for 40 minutes until the vegetables are cooked.
5. Add the **beans**.

Enjoy this soup with your favourite crusty bread. Experiment with different vegetables such as butternut squash, red peppers, sweet potato and add 1oz (25g) of lentils with the stock. Look out for bags of pre-prepared vegetables for soup when you are shopping.

Ingredients

1 small onion or shallot, finely chopped

1 small stick celery, sliced

1 carrot, sliced

½ thin leek, sliced

1 medium potato, peeled and cubed

1 clove garlic, finely chopped (optional)

1 (400g) tin tomatoes

300ml (½ pint) vegetable stock

Seasoning

1 small tin of beans (kidney beans, black eyed beans) (optional)

2 teaspoons olive oil

Lentil soup (V)

Preparation time 5-10 minutes

Cooking time 50 minutes to 1 hour

Method

1. Heat the **olive oil** in a heavy based pan.
2. Add the **carrots, potatoes, onions** and **garlic**. Stir over a medium heat for 5 minutes.
3. Add the **lentils, stock** and **seasoning.**
4. Bring to the boil (stirring occasionally). Turn the heat low, cover and leave to cook for 45 minutes until the vegetables are cooked.
5. Blend until smooth or serve as it is.

Ingredients (Serves 4)

200g (8oz) red lentils

2 carrots, sliced

200g (8oz) or 4 small potatoes, sliced

1 onion, chopped

1 clove of garlic, finely chopped

1 litre (2 pints) of vegetable or chicken stock

Seasoning

2 teaspoons olive oil

The soup can be kept in the fridge for up to a week. Remember to thoroughly reheat each time.
Freeze portions of soup in plastic containers, this makes it easy to have a healthier lunch or dinner when you are pushed for time.

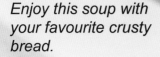

Enjoy this soup with your favourite crusty bread.

17

Prawn open sandwich

Preparation time 10 minutes

Cooking time 3 minutes

The prawn and salad mixture makes a great low fat topping for a jacket potato. Also makes a delicious filling for a wholemeal bun, wrap or toasted pitta bread.

Method

1. Make the dressing in a medium bowl. Mix the **mayonnaise, ketchup**, the juice from 4 of the **lemon** wedges and some **seasoning**.

2. Toss the **prawns, cucumber** and **tomatoes** in the dressing.

3. Toast the **bread** in a toaster or under the grill until golden brown.

4. Arrange the bread on a plate, top with **rocket** and spoon on the prawn filling.

5. Serve with the remaining **lemon** wedge and squeeze the juice over the prawn filling.

Ingredients

1 tablespoon low fat mayonnaise

2 teaspoons ketchup

½ lemon cut into 5 wedges

25g (1oz) ready cooked prawns

¼ cucumber, sliced

60g (2oz) cherry tomatoes, halved

A few leaves of rocket or lettuce

1 slice of wholemeal bread

Seasoning

Spicy beans on toast (V)

Preparation time 5 minutes

Cooking time 10 minutes

Method

1. Heat the **olive oil** in a small pan, add the **onion**, and gently cook until softened.

2. Sprinkle the **spices** into the pan and stir briefly to toast them.

3. Add the **sun-dried tomatoes** and **baked beans** and warm through.

4. Whilst the beans are warming, toast the **wholemeal bread** in a toaster or under the grill.

5. When the bread is toasted, place on a plate then pour the spiced beans over the top.

Ingredients

½ small onion or shallot, finely sliced

A pinch of ground cumin

A pinch of ground coriander

40g (1½oz) sun-dried tomatoes in oil, chopped

200g (8oz) can of reduced salt and sugar baked beans

2 slices of wholemeal bread

2 teaspoons olive oil

These beans are also a great accompaniment to a jacket potato.

Try serving with a poached egg on top for a more filling meal.

Mushroom and cheese toast (V)

Preparation time 5 minutes

Cooking time 5 minutes

Accompany with wedges of tomato.

Method

1. Toast the **bread** in a toaster or under the grill.
2. Spread the **chutney** onto the toast.
3. Place **mushroom** slices on top followed by the **cheese.**
4. Grill until cheese is bubbling and golden brown.

Alternatively prepare a sandwich and grill until the cheese has melted.

Ingredients

1 thick slice of bread (try wholemeal or granary bread)

1 teaspoon chutney

1 medium sized mushroom, sliced

50g (2oz) cheese, sliced (or a pre-pack slice)

Apple and cheese toast (V)

Preparation time 5 minutes

Cooking time 5 minutes

Method

1. Toast the **wholemeal bread** in a toaster or under the grill.
2. While it is toasting, combine the grated **apple,** grated **cheese, milk** and **mustard powder** (if using) in a bowl.
3. Place the topping onto the toast (use a fork to press it down).
4. Grill until cheese is melting and golden brown.

Ingredients

1 thick slice of bread (try wholemeal or granary bread)

½ eating apple, grated

50g (2oz) cheese, grated

1 teaspoon fresh milk

A pinch of mustard powder (optional)

21

Jacket potato and suggested fillings (V)

Preparation time 5 minutes

Cooking time 1 hour

Method

Oven only

1. Preheat oven to Gas 6/400°F/200°C (fan 180°C).
2. Wash and dry the **potato**.
3. Prick over surface with a sharp knife or fork.
4. Cook for about 1 hour.
5. Cut in half lengthwise and add chosen filling.

Or use a microwave

1. Prick the **potato** with a sharp knife and cook in a microwave for 5-7 minutes on a high setting depending on size of potato.
2. Transfer to a hot oven Gas 6/400°F/200°C (fan 180°C).
3. Cook for 25–30 minutes.
4. Cut in half lengthwise and add chosen filling.

Ingredients

1 baking potato

Suggested fillings:
- Cooked leeks and bacon
- Grated cheese and pickle / tomatoes (V)
- Coleslaw (V)
- Tuna and sweetcorn
- Prawns in mayonnaise (see page 18)
- Spicy beans (V) (see page 19)
- Mixed bean chilli (V) (see page 36)
- Spaghetti Bolognese (see page 38)

Tuna Nicoise salad

Preparation time 15 minutes

Cooking time 20 minutes

Method

1. Tear the **salad leaves** into bite-sized pieces and place in a large serving bowl.
2. Drain the tin of **tuna** and flake onto the salad leaves.
3. Add the **beans, tomatoes, potatoes, olives** and **anchovies**.
4. Place the **mustard, oil** reserved from the tuna and the **white wine vinegar** into a bowl, season and whisk well.
5. Pour over the salad and serve immediately.

Ingredients

- 25g (1oz) mixed salad leaves
- ½ small Gem lettuce (optional)
- 80g (3oz) tin of tuna in olive oil, drained but with oil reserved
- 100g (4oz) cannellini beans or similar (tinned or frozen)
- 2 tomatoes, chopped
- 4 cooked new potatoes
- ½ handful black olives
- ¼ small tin anchovies in olive oil
- ¼ teaspoon Dijon mustard
- 1 tablespoon olive oil, reserved when draining the tuna / anchovies
- ½ tablespoon white wine vinegar

Other tinned fish such as salmon also works well.

Try adding some sliced beetroot or grated carrot to the salad to give it some extra colour and increase the amount of vegetables. Try adding a drizzle of balsamic vinegar to the dish to give it a kick.

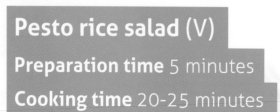

Pesto rice salad (V)

Preparation time 5 minutes

Cooking time 20-25 minutes

Serve with cooked meat or poultry and salad vegetables to make a complete meal.

Try this with different types of rice such as arborio, brown or long grain rice.

Ingredients

40g (1½oz) basmati rice

1½ teaspoons of pesto (see page 11)

200ml (8 fl oz) boiling water

Squeeze of lemon juice

1 tomato, chopped into small pieces

Seasoning

Method

1. Place **rice**, 1 teaspoon of **pesto** and **water** into a pan. Simmer for 20 minutes stirring frequently.
2. When cooked, stir in **lemon juice, seasoning** and ½ teaspoon of **extra pesto** for flavour.
3. When cold, add the **tomato** pieces.

Chicken salad

Preparation time 5-10 minutes

Method

1. Coat the **chicken** in the **pesto**, if using.
2. Serve the chicken, **salad (celery, carrot, pepper, sultanas)** and **coleslaw** separately or combine all the ingredients together.

Ingredients

75g (3oz) cooked chicken pieces

3 teaspoons of pesto (optional) (see page 11)

½ apple, chopped into small pieces

1 stick celery, chopped into small pieces

1 small carrot, grated (optional)

¼ red or yellow pepper, deseeded and diced

1 heaped tablespoon sultanas

1 heaped tablespoon coleslaw

A handful of lettuce leaves

Enjoy with toasted wholemeal bread.

Chicken and potato salad
Preparation time 10 minutes

This salad can be served hot or cold.

Try it with grated carrot, tomatoes or beetroot.
A boiled egg will give you extra protein.

Method
1. Put the **chicken** in a bowl.
2. Add the **potatoes, green beans, sultanas, tomato** and **lettuce leaves**.
3. Combine the **lemon juice, olive oil** and **seasoning** to make a salad dressing. Toss with the salad.

Ingredients
75g (3oz) cooked chicken, cut into bite size pieces

3 cooked new potatoes (warm or cold)

6 cooked whole green beans (or 1 tablespoon of peas or sweetcorn)

1 dessert spoon sultanas

1 tomato, cut into chunks or 3 cherry tomatoes, halved

Handful of lettuce leaves

Squeeze of lemon juice

2 teaspoons olive oil

Seasoning

Couscous salad (V)
Preparation time 10 minutes

Method

1. Place the **couscous, lemon juice,** and **olive oil** in a bowl. Pour in the **boiling water** and stir.
2. Cover bowl with cling film and leave for 15 minutes.
3. Add the **tomato, cucumber, sultanas** and **herbs.**

Also try using bulgar wheat or quinoa instead of couscous. Cook as directed on the packaging.

Delicious on its own or serve with cooked meat, poultry or fish.

Ingredients

25g (1oz) couscous

A squeeze of lemon juice

½ tablespoon olive oil

50ml (2 fl oz) boiling water

1 tomato, cut into chunks or 3 cherry tomatoes, halved

Cucumber, cut in small pieces

1 tablespoon sultanas

1 teaspoon freshly chopped mint or parsley

This also works well with nectarines, pomegranate seeds, fresh or dried ready to eat apricots or dried cranberries, flaked almonds or toasted hazelnuts.

Broad bean, barley & mint salad (V)

Preparation time 15-20 minutes

Cooking time 1 hour

The salad can be refrigerated for one to two days.

Serve with cooked meat dishes or on its own.

Method

1. Heat the **stock** in a medium saucepan until boiling then add the **broad beans** and cook for 3 minutes or until they float. Remove from the pan using a slotted spoon, transfer to a bowl and leave to cool.

2. Add the **pearl barley** to the stock and simmer over a low heat for 40 minutes until tender. Drain the barley, stir through the **whole mint** leaves, then leave to cool.

3. Whisk the **olive oil, vinegar, lemon juice** and **chopped mint** leaves together.

4. Season and stir into the barley. Add the broad beans.

5. Serve onto individual plates, scatter with the **radishes** and **hazelnuts,** and crumble over the **goat's cheese.**

Ingredients

250ml (10 fl oz) vegetable stock

125g (5oz) podded broad beans or peas (fresh, tinned or frozen)

50g (2oz) pearl barley

Small handful of mint leaves (whole)

1 tablespoon of olive oil

1 teaspoon of red wine vinegar

Juice of ½ a lemon

Heaped teaspoon of finely chopped mint leaves

50g (2oz) radishes, quartered

25g (1oz) whole hazelnuts, roughly chopped

15g (½oz) goat's cheese

Vegetable rice salad (V)

Preparation time 10 minutes

Cooking time 30 minutes

Method

1. Add the **rice** to boiling water in a pan. Bring to the boil, uncovered. Cover with a lid and simmer for 15-20 minutes until cooked (if using white rice reduce the cooking time to 10 minutes).

2. Mix in the **peas, pepper, tomato, spring onion, parsley** and **olives** (if using).

3. Stir through the **mayonnaise, lemon juice** and **olive oil** and **season** to taste.

Ingredients

50g (2oz) uncooked brown rice

25g (1oz) peas, fresh (or frozen and defrosted)

¼ pepper, sliced and deseeded

1 tomato, chopped into chunks

1 spring onion, finely sliced

1 tablespoon parsley, chopped

4 olives, stoned and halved (optional)

2 teaspoons mayonnaise

Juice of ¼ of a lemon

1 teaspoon olive oil

Seasoning

Serve with cooked meat, chicken or fish.

Carrots with orange or lemon (V)

Preparation time 5 minutes

Cooking time 10-15 minutes

A great way to get Vitamin C.

Method

1. Cook **carrots** until tender, drain away water.
2. Add some zest and a squeeze of juice from an **orange** or **lemon**.
3. Return to the heat for 1 minute.

Ingredients

1 carrot, peeled and sliced

1 small orange or lemon (zest and juice)

Parsnip and potato mash (V)

Preparation time 5 minutes

Cooking time 15-20 minutes

Ingredients

1 medium parsnip

1 medium potato (variety for mashing)

Seasoning

Method

1. Peel and cut the **potato** and **parsnip** into small pieces.

2. Add the potatoes to the pan and bring to the boil. After 5 minutes add the parsnip. Cook for around 15-20 minutes until the potato pieces fall off a sharp knife when pricked.

3. When cooked, drain. Leave for a couple of minutes to release some steam. This ensures the mash is not too wet. Mash with a potato masher until there are virtually no lumps.

4. Add **seasoning** to taste.

To make aromatic Mediterranean mash, add a tablespoon of olive oil and some fresh herbs such as rosemary or garlic.

For a tasty alternative try mashing potato with sweet potato, spring onions or finely shredded cabbage.

Any mash left over can be saved and used in fishcakes or to top a shepherd's or fish pie.

Roasted vegetables (V)
Preparation time 5-10 minutes
Cooking time 35-40 minutes

Try adding herbs such as rosemary, oregano or thyme with the olive oil to increase the flavour.

Other vegetables that work well include butternut squash and mushrooms.

Method

1. In a large bowl, combine the **pepper, carrot, parsnip, onion** and **sweet potato**.

2. In a small bowl, stir together **olive oil, vinegar** and a pinch of **seasoning.**

3. Toss with vegetables until they are coated. Spread evenly on a large roasting pan.

4. Roast for 35-40 minutes in the preheated oven Gas 4/350°F/180°C (fan 160°C.), stirring every 15 minutes, or until vegetables are cooked through and browned.

Ingredients
½ pepper, deseeded and sliced
½ carrot, sliced lengthways
½ parsnip, sliced lengthways
½ small onion or shallot
½ sweet potato, cut into wedges
2 teaspoons balsamic vinegar
1 tablespoon of olive oil
Seasoning

Roasted vegetable lasagne (V)

Preparation time 15 minutes

Cooking time 1 hour

Method

1. Preheat the oven to Gas 4/350°F/180°C (fan 160°C.) Toss the **olive oil** and **aubergine, onion, pepper, tomatoes** and **garlic** together and roast in a large, shallow tin for 35 minutes until lightly charred.

2. Spoon a layer of roasted vegetables over the bottom of a small baking dish.

3. Pour over some **passata** and cover with a layer of **lasagne** sheets.

4. Repeat layers to use up all the roasted vegetables and passata, finishing with a layer of lasagne.

5. Use a spoon to dollop over the **crème fraîche**, and then sprinkle with the **parmesan or cheddar.**

6. Return to the oven for 25 minutes, until the lasagne is cooked through and the top is golden and bubbling.

Ingredients (serves 2)

1 small onion or shallot, sliced

½ aubergine, cut into chunks

½ pepper, deseeded and sliced

4 tomatoes halved

1 small garlic clove, sliced

175ml (6oz) passata

100g (4oz) ready cooked lasagne sheets

3 tablespoons of half fat crème fraiche (or fat free quark)

25g (1oz) parmesan or cheddar, grated

1 tablespoon olive oil

The lasagne can be frozen in portions and defrosted as required.

Try using wholemeal lasagne sheets. Try using different vegetables to add colour to the dish such as courgette and mushrooms. Try using a strong cheddar cheese, this means you will still be able to taste it even if you are using a small amount.

Roasted vegetable tagine with couscous (V)

Preparation time 10-15 minutes
Cooking time 45 minutes

Method

1. Heat oven to Gas 6/400°F/200°C (fan 180°C). Scatter the **carrot, parsnip, onion** and **pepper** on a baking tray, drizzle with half the **olive oil** and **season**. Stir to coat the vegetables. Roast for 30 minutes until tender and beginning to brown.

2. 25 minutes after the vegetables have gone into the oven, put the **couscous** in a bowl and pour on the hot vegetable **stock** (use water that has very recently been boiled). Cover with a lid or plate and leave to stand for 10 minutes.

3. Meanwhile, fry the **cumin, paprika, cinnamon** and **chilli** in the remaining **olive oil** for 1 minute – they should sizzle and start to smell aromatic. Add the **tomatoes, chickpeas, apricots, honey** and 100ml (4 fl oz) of **water**. Simmer for 5 minutes until the sauce is slightly reduced and the apricots plump, then stir in the vegetables, the coriander and some seasoning.

4. Fluff up the couscous with a fork and drizzle over a little extra olive oil, if desired. Serve.

Ingredients

1 carrot, cut into chunks

1 small parsnip, cut into chunks

1 small red onion, cut in wedges

½ red pepper, deseeded and cut into chunks

A pinch of ground cumin

A pinch of paprika

A pinch of cinnamon

A pinch of chilli powder

100g (4oz) tinned chopped tomatoes

100g (4oz) tinned chickpeas, drained

1–2 soft dried ready to eat apricots

1 teaspoon honey

100ml (4 fl oz) of water

50g (2oz) couscous

60ml (2 fl oz) hot vegetable stock

1 tablespoon olive oil

Seasoning

Fresh coriander to garnish

Vegetable risotto (V)

Preparation time 10 minutes

Cooking time 25-30minutes

Method

1. Heat the **olive oil** in a large non-stick saucepan and fry the **onion** and **garlic** for five minutes until softened, but not coloured. Stir in the **thyme, bay leaf** and **risotto rice** and cook (stirring constantly) for about a minute more until the rice is glistening.

2. Pour the **wine** into the pan and boil over a medium heat until the liquid has reduced by half. Slowly start adding the **stock**, a ladleful at a time, stirring well between each addition. Simmer for 2-3 minutes or until the liquid has almost all been absorbed, before adding more. Cook for 20 minutes or until the rice is close to tender but still slightly grainy in the centre.

3. Stir in the **runner beans, spinach, peas** and **asparagus** with the remaining stock and cook for 7-10 minutes until tender, stirring regularly. Remove from the heat and stir in the **feta cheese**. Season.

Ingredients

¼ onion, finely chopped

1 garlic clove, crushed

A pinch of dried thyme

1 bay leaf

75g (3oz) Arborio risotto rice (pudding rice also works)

50ml (2 fl oz) dry white wine

175ml (7 fl oz) hot vegetable stock

25g (1oz) fresh runner beans, de-stringed

50g (2oz) spinach, roughly torn

25g (1oz) peas (fresh or frozen)

50g (2oz) asparagus, trimmed and snapped in half

25g (1oz) feta cheese, drained and crumbled into small pieces

1 teaspoon olive oil

Try substituting the vegetables with a mixture of different kinds of mushrooms.

Mixed bean chilli (V)
Preparation time 15 minutes
Cooking time 25 minutes

The Chilli can be frozen in batches in the freezer or kept in the fridge for up to a week.

*Makes a great topping for a jacket potato.
Serve in wholemeal wraps with crunchy lettuce and cucumber strips.
Try adding other vegetables to the dish. Courgettes and aubergines work well.*

Method

1. Put the **olive oil** into a casserole dish and fry the **onion, garlic** and **pepper** for 5 minutes.
2. Add **Cajun spice, pulses, tomato puree, tinned tomatoes** and **stock**. Cover and simmer for 15–20 minutes.
3. Serve in a bowl, and top with the **yoghurt** and a squeeze of **lime** if desired.
4. Serve with **rice** or **crusty bread**.

Ingredients

2 teaspoons olive oil

1 small onion or shallot, chopped

1 small clove garlic, chopped

½ yellow pepper, deseeded and diced

2 teaspoons Cajun spice (or 1 teaspoon each of cayenne pepper and paprika)

2 teaspoons tomato puree

½ a 230g (10oz) tin mixed pulses (such as chickpeas, black eyed beans, pinto beans, haricot beans, red kidney beans, adzuki beans) in water, rinsed and drained

100g can chopped tomatoes

50ml (2 fl oz) vegetable stock

2 teaspoons low fat or fat free Greek yoghurt

Wedges of lime (to serve, optional)

50g–75g (2–3oz) rice (brown rice if you have it) or crusty bread

Corned beef hash

Preparation time 10 minutes

Cooking time 20 minutes

Method

1. Heat the **oil** in a small pan and add the **onions.** Cook for 1 minute.
2. Add the **potatoes** and **carrots** and stir.
3. Add **stock, seasoning** and **Worcester sauce.** Simmer for 10-15 minutes until the vegetables are tender.
4. Add the **corned beef** and stir in to warm it through.
5. You can place it under the grill to brown if desired.

Ingredients

1 small onion or shallot, chopped

1 large potato, peeled and cubed

1 carrot, sliced

100ml (4 fl oz) beef stock

Seasoning

A dash of Worcester sauce

100g (4oz) corned beef, cut into cubes or strips

2 teaspoons olive oil

Serve with a selection of vegetables of your choice.

Spaghetti Bolognese

Preparation time 10-15 minutes

Cooking time 45 minutes

Method

1. Heat a large deep frying pan and add the **olive oil**. Add the **mince** and fry over a high heat until browned, breaking it up using a wooden spoon.
2. Add the **onion, carrots, celery** and **garlic**. Stir over a medium heat for 5 minutes. Add in the **wine** (if using) and cook for a further minute.
3. Add the **chopped tomatoes, tomato puree**, crumble in the **beef stock cube** and stir in the **thyme, rosemary** and **bay leaf**. Add **seasoning**.
4. Cook over a medium heat uncovered so that the sauce simmers gently, stirring occasionally, for 30 minutes or until thickened.
5. While the sauce is cooking, cook the **spaghetti (or pasta shapes)** in a pan of salted boiling water for 10 minutes, or according to the pack instructions, until tender with a bite at the centre. Drain and turn into a warmed serving bowl.
6. Taste the sauce, adjust the seasoning and remove the bay leaf. Pour the sauce over the pasta and toss gently. Serve immediately with **grated parmesan cheese**.

Ingredients (serves 2)

175g (7oz) lean minced beef

1 large onion, finely chopped

2 medium carrots, peeled and finely chopped

2 celery sticks, finely chopped

1 garlic clove, crushed

50ml (2 fl oz) red wine (optional)

1 (400g) tin chopped tomatoes

1 tablespoon tomato puree

Beef stock cube

A pinch of dried thyme

A pinch of dried rosemary

1 bay leaf

Seasoning

100g (4oz) dried spaghetti (or pasta shapes of your choice)

10g (½oz) grated Parmesan cheese, to serve

2 teaspoons olive oil

Cottage pie

Preparation time 20 minutes

Cooking time 1 hour

Method

1. Preheat oven to Gas 6/400°F/200°C (fan 180°C).
2. Peel and cut the **potato** into small pieces. Add to a pan of boiling water and simmer for 10-15 minutes until soft.
3. Heat the **olive oil** in a small pan and add the **onion** and **carrot**. Cook for 2-3 minutes stirring continuously.
4. Add the **mince** and cook for 2 minutes stirring continuously.
5. Turn off heat and stir in the **flour.**
6. Gradually stir in the **beef stock** then return to heat and stir until thickened.
7. Place mince in a small ovenproof dish.
8. Drain and mash the potatoes and place on top of mince. Top with **cheese.**
9. Bake for 20-25 minutes.

Ingredients

1 large potato

1 small onion or shallot, chopped

1 small carrot, sliced

100g (4oz) minced beef

1 teaspoon plain flour

Seasoning

100ml (3 fl oz) beef stock

40g (1½oz) cheddar or other hard cheese, grated

2 teaspoons olive oil

Serve with a selection of vegetables of your choice. Try the recipe for carrots with orange or lemon (see page 30).

Baked chicken with olive oil and lemon

Preparation time 25 minutes

Cooking time 30 minutes

Skinless chicken legs and thighs are a cheaper alternative to chicken breast. Turkey breasts can also be used.

Serve with a side salad, vegetable rice salad (see page 29) or roasted vegetables (see page 32) and parsnip and potato mash (see page 31).

Method

1. Combine **oil, lemon juice, garlic, oregano** and **rosemary**; pour over **chicken**.
2. Preheat oven to Gas 4/350°F/180°C (fan 160°C).
3. Cover and place in the fridge to marinate for 20 minutes.
4. Bake the chicken for 25-30 minutes or until the juices run clear and the chicken is white throughout. Baste frequently during baking.

Ingredients

1 tablespoon olive oil

2 tablespoons lemon juice

1 clove of garlic, finely chopped

A pinch of dried oregano

A pinch of dried rosemary

1 skinless chicken breast halved

Chicken burgers

Preparation time 10 minutes

Cooking time 10 minutes

Method

1. Heat grill to high. Put the **chicken** breast between 2 pieces of cling film and flatten with a rolling pin until it is about half the original thickness.

2. Use a blender or food processor to break the **bread** into rough breadcrumbs. Tip out onto a plate.

3. Beat the **egg** and **mustard** together in a bowl and season.

4. Dip the chicken into the egg, let the excess drip back into the bowl, and then press into the breadcrumbs.

5. Put under the grill on a flat baking sheet and grill for about 10 minutes, turning once, until golden and crisp on both sides and the chicken is cooked through.

6. Beat the **lemon zest, lemon juice** and **black pepper** into the **mayonnaise.**

7. Spread some of the mayonnaise onto the bottom halves of the **bread bun,** top with the chicken breast and serve.

Ingredients

1 chicken breast

1 slice of stale wholemeal bread

1 egg

2 teaspoons Dijon or English mustard

Zest and juice of ¼ lemon

1 teaspoon reduced fat mayonnaise

Black pepper

1 wholemeal bread bun

Try cutting the chicken into strips to make chicken goujons. Serve with oven chips cooked in olive oil and peas.

Add some crunchy lettuce leaves and tomatoes to your burger buns to increase your vegetable intake.

Chicken, spinach and potato frittata

Preparation time 5 minutes

Cooking time 25 minutes

Enjoy with a crispy side salad.

Method

1. Heat half of the **olive oil** in a small non-stick frying pan, add the diced **potatoes**, and sliced **onion**. Cook for approximately 5 minutes until they have browned. Reduce the heat and cook for 10 minutes, stirring continuously until the potatoes are cooked.
2. Add the **chicken** and cook for a further 2 minutes.
3. Add the **spinach** and **seasoning** and cook for a further 2 minutes.
4. Add remaining **olive oil** to the pan. Turn up heat and add the **beaten eggs**. Reduce heat after 2 minutes. Continue to cook over a low heat until the top has set.

Ingredients

1 medium (100g/4oz) potato, peeled and diced into small pieces

1 small onion or shallot, sliced

100g (4oz) cooked chicken breast, cut into small pieces

Handful of baby spinach leaves

Seasoning

2 eggs, beaten

1 tablespoon olive oil

Chicken hotpot

Preparation time 5-10 minutes

Cooking time 50-55 minutes

Method

1. Heat the **olive oil** in a small heavy based pan.
2. Add the **chicken** and cook for 2-3 minutes on each side.
3. Add the **onion, celery, carrot, garlic** and **bacon**. Stir over the heat for further 2 minutes.
4. Add the **stock** and bring to the boil.
5. Top with **sliced potatoes.**
6. Put lid on pan and leave to simmer for 45 minutes. Or cook in a casserole dish in the oven at Gas 3/325°F/160°C (fan 140°C) for 45 minutes.

Ingredients

1 chicken leg or small breast

½ small onion or shallot, chopped

1 small stick celery, sliced

1 small carrot, sliced

1 small clove garlic, chopped

1 rasher of bacon, chopped

300ml (½ pint) chicken stock

1 large potato, sliced

1 teaspoon olive oil

Baked fish and chips

Preparation time 15 minutes

Cooking time 40-45 minutes

If you are on a budget try looking for cheaper cuts of fish such as pollock, it is just as tasty.

For an alternative serve the fish with mashed potato and peas.

Method

1. Preheat oven to Gas 6/400°F/200°C (fan 180°C). Put the peeled, whole **potatoes** in a saucepan, cover with boiling water and cook gently for 3 minutes.
2. Drain, and then dry the potatoes on kitchen paper. Cut each potato lengthways into slices about 2cm (¾in) thick, and then cut each slice into two or three thick wedges.
3. Brush a non-stick baking tray with **some of the olive oil.** Then spread the chips onto the tray. Bake for 35 minutes, turning them over halfway through cooking.
4. Meanwhile, prepare the **fish**. Lightly oil another non-stick baking tray. Lay the fillet, skin side down, on the tray. Spread a teaspoon of the **mayonnaise** over the fillet.
5. Mix together the **breadcrumbs, spread, cheese, parsley** and **season** to taste. Spread the mixture evenly over the fish, pressing it in gently.
6. Bake the fish on the middle shelf of the oven for the final 10-15 minutes of the chips' cooking time. To serve, garnish with **fresh parsley** and **lemon** wedge.

Ingredients

150g (6oz) baking potatoes, peeled

1 teaspoon olive oil

1 small fillet of cod or haddock, about 125g (5oz)

1 teaspoon reduced-fat mayonnaise

15g (½oz) fresh white breadcrumbs

1 teaspoon low fat spread, melted

1 teaspoon grated Parmesan cheese

1 teaspoon chopped fresh parsley

Seasoning

Sprigs of fresh flat-leaved parsley

1 wedge of lemon

Cod and tomato tray bake

Preparation time 10 minutes

Cooking time 30 minutes

Method

1. Heat oven to Gas 7/425°F/ 220°C (fan 200°C).
2. Put the **pepper, onions, olives** and **tomatoes** into a large, deep baking tray then drizzle with the **olive oil.**
3. Toss the vegetables until coated in the olive oil and cook for 15 minutes.
4. Remove from the oven and stir the chopped **tomatoes, butter beans** and **seasoning** into the vegetables.
5. Make a well in the tomato sauce to nestle the **cod fillet** in. Return to the oven and cook for a further 15 minutes or until the cod is cooked through.
6. Sprinkle with the **basil leaves** and serve.

Try adding ½ teaspoon of chilli powder for a spicy alternative.

Ingredients

½ red pepper, deseeded and sliced

½ red onion, sliced

50g (2oz) cherry tomatoes

4 black olives (optional)

100g (4oz) tinned chopped tomatoes

200g (8oz) tinned butter beans

1 skinless cod fillet (150g / 6oz)

Small handful of fresh basil

Seasoning

2 teaspoons olive oil

If you are on a budget try looking for cheaper cuts of fish such as pollock, it's just as tasty. Prawns also work really well as a substitute for the cod.

Serve on its own or with some crusty wholemeal bread.

Salmon parcel with leeks and parsley sauce

Preparation time 15 minutes

Cooking time 20-25 minutes

Method

1. Lightly grease with **olive oil** a square of aluminium foil (large enough to wrap the fish in).

2. Sprinkle **lemon rind** and **seasoning** onto foil and place the **salmon** on top. Lay the **leeks** on top of the salmon. Wrap into a sealed parcel.

3. Bring a pan of water to boil and place in **potatoes.** Lay the fish parcel on top. Cook for 15-20 minutes.

4. Meanwhile make the parsley sauce. Melt the **low fat spread** in a saucepan.

5. Stir in the **flour** and cook for 1-2 minutes.

6. Take the pan off the heat and gradually stir in the **milk** to get a smooth sauce.

7. Return to the heat and, stirring all the time, bring to the boil. Simmer gently, stirring continuously until the sauce thickens. **Season** to taste.

8. When potatoes are cooked remove fish parcel, open and serve with drained potatoes.

9. Stir the **parsley** into the sauce and serve.

Ingredients

1 teaspoon olive oil

Grated lemon rind

Seasoning

1 salmon steak, fillet or pieces of salmon

2 baby leeks, sliced lengthwise or ½ leek cut into rings

Potatoes and vegetables of your choice

15g (½oz) low fat spread

15g (½oz) plain flour

300ml (½ pint milk)

Seasoning

2 tablespoons parsley, freshly chopped

Smoked mackerel paté
Preparation time 5 minutes

Method
1. Remove the skin and bones from **mackerel.**
2. Place fish in bowl and mash with a fork.
3. Add the **soft cheese** and **lemon juice**. Mix until smooth.

Try swapping the mackerel for smoked salmon. Use the salt free seasoning (see page 10) to enhance flavour or add a little horseradish sauce.

Ingredients
1 moist fillet smoked mackerel
  (about 75g or 3oz)
100g (4oz) low fat soft cheese
  (half of a 200g container)
Juice of half a small lemon

Keeps well, covered, in the refrigerator for 2 days.

Tasty spread on toast with a small salad.

Tuna pasta bake

Preparation time 15 minutes

Cooking time 20 minutes

A simple side salad of lettuce, cucumber and tomatoes makes a good accompaniment to the pasta bake.

Any leftover bake can be frozen and defrosted/reheated in the microwave.

Why not try using different combinations of vegetables, try adding other colourful vegetables such as leeks, grated carrot, tinned sweet corn and butternut squash. Adding basil to the dish will also give it some extra flavour.

Adding chopped cooked chicken to the dish is also a nice alternative to tuna.

Method

1. Preheat oven to Gas 5/375°F/190°C (fan 170°C).
2. Heat the **olive oil** in a pan, add the **onion, pepper** and **mushrooms** and cook for a couple of minutes.
3. Stir in the **garlic, tomatoes** and **chilli powder** and bring to the boil.
4. Give it a good stir, then reduce the heat and simmer for 5 minutes.
5. Meanwhile, bring a large pan of salted water to the boil. Add the **pasta** and cook according to packet instructions.
6. Flake the **tuna** into the sauce and heat through.
7. Drain the pasta, return to the pan and stir in the sauce and **basil leaves** if you have any.
8. Add to an oven proof dish and sprinkle over the grated **cheese.**
9. Put under the grill until the cheese is bubbling then serve.

Ingredients

1 small onion or shallot, chopped

½ red, yellow or green pepper, deseeded and chopped

25g (1oz) mushrooms, chopped

1 small garlic clove, finely chopped

100g (8oz) tinned chopped tomatoes

A pinch of chilli powder

75 (3oz) of pasta shapes

1 small tin tuna fish in brine or fresh water, drained

1 tablespoon reduced fat cheddar cheese, grated

A handful of fresh basil leaves

2 teaspoons olive oil

Devilled liver and onions

Preparation time 5 minutes

Cooking time 10 minutes

Method

1. Heat **1 teaspoon of olive oil** in a small non-stick frying pan, add **onions** and cook until soft.
2. Meanwhile, dust the **liver** in the seasoned **flour.**
3. Remove onions from pan.
4. Add **1 teaspoon of olive oil** to the pan and cook the liver over a medium heat for 2–3 minutes each side until nearly cooked.
5. Pour enough water (or vegetable cooking liquid) to cover base of pan. Mix in **mustard** and turn the liver slices in this gravy to thicken it.
6. Place onions back over liver and cook all together for 1 minute.

Serve with potatoes and vegetables of your choice.

Ingredients

80g (3oz) thinly cut lamb's liver

1 onion, sliced into rings

15g (½oz) seasoned flour

½ teaspoon French mustard

2 teaspoons olive oil

Great with carrots with orange or lemon (see page 30) or parsnip and potato mash (see page 31)

Pork chop with apples

Preparation time 5 minutes

Cooking time 15 minutes

Great with carrots with orange or lemon (see page 30) or parsnip and potato mash (see page 31).

Method

1. Cook the **pork chop** in a non-stick frying pan, cook for 5 minutes on each side. Add **seasoning**.
2. Add the **apple** and **onion** to the pan, cook in the pork juices.
3. When chop is cooked through add the liquid to the pan and continue cooking for 2-3 minutes.
4. Serve with potatoes and vegetables.

Ingredients

1 pork chop

½ eating apple, chopped finely

½ onion, chopped finely

110ml (4 fl oz) cider or apple juice

Seasoning

Sardinian stew

Preparation time 10-15 minutes

Cooking time 35-40 minutes

Method

1. For the sauce, heat the **olive oil** in a casserole dish or large pan, add the **onion,** and let it cook for 5 minutes over a moderate heat until softened.
2. Add the **garlic** and cook for another minute before adding the **salami/pepperoni/chorizo, mushrooms** and **pepper.**
3. Allow to brown, stirring, and then pour in the **wine** and the **passata.**
4. Add the **rosemary** and **pearl barley** then leave to cook over a very low heat for about 30 minutes.
5. If more moisture is needed, add a little more white wine or just water.
6. When ready, season to taste, fish out the sprigs of rosemary and enjoy with a leafy salad.

Ingredients

1 small onion or shallot, chopped

1 small garlic clove, chopped

10g thinly sliced then chopped salami, pepperoni or chorizo

25g (1oz) mushrooms, sliced

½ red pepper, deseeded and chopped

1 tablespoon dry white wine

150g (6oz) passata (or chopped tomatoes)

2 teaspoons dried rosemary

75g quick-cook pearl barley

Seasoning

1 tablespoon olive oil

Pearl barley is also known as faro; if you can't find quick-cook then boil the pearl barley in water for about 15 minutes before starting.

Make it different: Orzo or other small pasta would be a good substitute for the pearl barley but you should reduce cooking time from 30 minutes to 20 minutes.

Stir fry greens with bacon

Preparation time 5 minutes

Cooking time 10 minutes

This is delicious with parsnip and potato mash (see page 31).

Method

1. Slice the **greens** finely and chop the **bacon** into small pieces.
2. Heat the **olive oil** in a heavy based pan.
3. Add the bacon and **onion.** Stir fry for 3-5 minutes until brown.
4. Add the greens and stir constantly until cooked (they will wilt but stay green)
5. Serve immediately.

Ingredients

200g (8oz) greens such as cabbage or sprouts

2 rashers back bacon

2 teaspoons olive oil

2 spring onions or small onion or shallot, chopped

Savoury rice with bacon

Preparation time 5 minutes

Cooking time 20-25 minutes

Method

1. Lightly cook the **bacon, onion, celery** and **garlic** with the **olive oil** in a pan for 2 minutes stirring continuously.
2. Add the **rice** and stir.
3. Immediately add **half the stock** and **parsley** and stir. Bring to the boil then turn down the heat.
4. Stir occasionally (adding **more stock** when mixture gets dry) for 20 minutes.
5. Add the **fresh parsley** when rice is cooked for added flavour and colour.

Ingredients

1 rasher bacon (fat removed), chopped

½ small onion or shallot, chopped

1 stick celery, chopped

1 clove garlic, chopped

1 heaped tablespoon rice (basmati is ideal)

300ml (½ pint) chicken stock

1 tablespoon fresh parsley, chopped **or** 1 teaspoon dried parsley

1 teaspoon of olive oil

Add extra bacon for a complete meal. Alternatively try adding pieces of cooked chicken for the last 5 minutes of cooking time.

Spice roasted fruits with honey and orange sauce (V)

Preparation time 5-10 minutes

Cooking time 25-30 minutes

The dish will store well for 3 to 4 days if kept covered and refrigerated.

Method

1. Preheat the oven Gas 6/400°F/200°C (fan 180°C).
2. Mix the **honey, orange juice** and **zest, cinnamon, bay leaf, vanilla** and **black pepper** together in a baking dish and set aside.
3. If using fresh fruit, cut the **peaches, pears** or **nectarines** in half and remove the stones then halve the **figs.** Place the fruit (fresh or tinned) in the baking dish and coat with the sauce. Turn all the fruits cut side up then dot with the **low fat spread.**
4. Roast the fruits for 10 minutes then remove from the oven and baste the fruits with the sauce. Roast again for 15 minutes, basting at least 3 times, until the fruits are tender.
5. Remove from the oven and serve with a drizzle of the sauce, a dollop of low fat or fat free **Greek yoghurt** and sprinkle of **granola** (if using).

Ingredients (serves 2)

2 teaspoons of clear honey

Zest and juice of 1 orange

A pinch cinnamon

1 bay leaf

A drop of vanilla extract

A pinch ground black pepper

2 fresh peaches, pears or nectarines (tinned also works fine too)

2 fresh figs (or 6 fresh plums or 6 tinned apricots)

1 teaspoon of low fat spread or olive oil spread

2 tablespoons low fat or fat free Greek yoghurt to serve

1 tablespoon granola to sprinkle on the top (optional)

54

Orchard fruit crumble (V)

Preparation time 5-10 minutes

Cooking time 30-45 minutes

Method

1. First make the topping. Add the **flour, oats** and the **low fat spread** into a large bowl. Rub the ingredients together until crumbs are formed. Do not worry if there are lumps as this will make it crunchier. Stir in the **sugar** then chill until needed.

2. Preheat oven to Gas 4/350°F/180°C (fan 160°C).

3. Add the chopped **apple** and **plums** to a large pan with the water. Cook for around 5–10 minutes until the apples are soft. Stir in the **blackberries, honey** and **cinnamon** and tip into a small baking dish.

4. Remove the topping from the fridge and scatter over the crumble and bake for 35 minutes. The top should be golden and the fruit should be bubbling.

5. Serve with **custard**, low fat or fat free Greek yoghurt or ice cream.

Alternatively use 100-110g (4oz) shop-bought crumble topping mix.

Ingredients (serves 2)

50g (2oz) self-raising flour (wholemeal if you have it)

25g (1oz) porridge oats

50g (2oz) low fat spread

25g (1oz) sugar (brown sugar if you have it)

1 eating apple, peeled, cored, cut into eight pieces (or pear)

2 plums, stoned and quartered

100g (4oz) blackberries (or other berries)

A pinch of cinnamon or mixed spice

2 teaspoons honey

25ml (1 fl oz) water

Custard, yoghurt or ice cream to serve

Crumble freezes really well so you can always have a dessert at the ready.

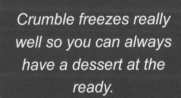

Baked apple with fruit (V)

Preparation time 5 minutes
Cooking time 20-30 minutes

Method

1. Preheat the oven to Gas 6/400°F/200°C (fan 180°C). Alternatively, this dish can be microwaved (high power for 5 minutes).
2. Grease a small baking dish with the **low fat spread.**
3. Mix the **sultanas, brown sugar, hazelnuts** and **cinnamon** together in a bowl.
4. Stand up the **apple** with its core removed in a baking dish. Using your fingers, push all the sultana mixture into the centre where the core was.
5. Cook in the oven for 20–30 minutes or until the apple has softened.
6. To serve place each apple into a bowl and spoon over any remaining juices.
7. Serve with **custard,** low fat or fat free Greek yoghurt or ice cream.

Ingredients

1 eating apple, core removed and scored around the circumference with a small, sharp knife

½ teaspoon low fat spread (or olive oil spread)

25g (1oz) sultanas (or cranberries or chopped dried apricots)

1 teaspoon sugar (use brown sugar if you have it)

A pinch of cinnamon (or mixed spice, nutmeg or ginger)

15g (½oz) hazelnuts, roughly chopped (or any chopped nuts)

Custard, yoghurt or ice cream to serve

Fruity bread and butter pudding (V)

Preparation time 10-15 minutes

Cooking time 30 minutes

Method

1. Pre-heat oven to gas 4/350°F/180°C (fan 160°C).
2. Lightly butter the **fruit loaf** with the **low fat spread** and cut into triangles.
3. Place into a shallow dish and sprinkle on the **dried fruit.**
4. Mix **egg** and **milk** together, pour over bread.
5. Allow to stand for 5 minutes before cooking.
6. Bake for 30 minutes until set.
7. Serve on its own or with **custard** or **ice-cream.**

Ingredients

2 slices fruit loaf

1 egg

200ml (7 fl oz) milk

2 teaspoons low fat spread

25g (1oz) dried sultanas/raisins

Custard or ice-cream to serve

Light and easy Eton mess (V)
Preparation time 5 minutes

You can make this to eat straight away or prepare just before your meal so the meringue is still crunchy.

Method

1. Break up the **meringue** nest in a bowl with the back of a spoon.
2. Place the **yoghurt**, meringue and **berries** in layers in a dish or tall glass tumbler

OR

3. Mix the broken meringue nest and yoghurt together before gently folding in the berries. Top with sliced strawberries, berries or crumbled meringue.

Ingredients

1 individual meringue nest

80g to 100g (3-4oz) fresh berries (or any frozen berries, defrosted)

125g low fat or fat free Greek yoghurt

Milk jelly and fruit

Preparation time 5 minutes

Cooking time 30 minutes - 1 hour

Method

1. Melt **jelly** with a little boiling water.
2. Make up to 300ml (½ pint) with **milk.**
3. Pour into two small bowls and add the **fruit**.
4. Refrigerate until set.

Ingredients (serves 2)

½ pack of fruit jelly

300ml (½ pint) milk

Fresh or tinned fruit, chopped
   up (strawberries, raspberries,
   blackberries, peaches)

This jelly will keep for 2 days in a covered dish in the fridge.